RUSSIA

LAND AND PEOPLE

LONDON & FLINT RIVER EDITIONS
GREAT BRITAIN

RUSSIA – LAND AND PEOPLE

370 Old Street
London EC1V 9LT

Produced in cooperation with "A.V. Tourow" Publishing Co.
Licence no. ЛР 064953 – 29 January 1997

ISBN: 5-89626-004-0 (Russian)
0-9530650-1-4 (UK)

General Director
Tom Wilson

Book originated and developed by
Bato Tomasevic

Text and captions
Madge Phillips

Design
Gane Aleksic

Editor
Karina Petrik

Photography
I. Gavrilov 21,47,57,65,90,91,97,101,105,112,114,122,123,129,156;
B. Golovchenko 117;
V. Gritsyuk 2-5,7,9,18,20,24,27,29-31,33,45,46,48-56,58-64,66-69,
71-81,83-89,92-96,98-100, 102-104,106,107,109,110,120,121,124,
131-147,150,151,157,160,164;
I. Keitelgisser/V. Nekrasov 1,6,12,14,15,34,35,37,39,40-43,158
V.Kornyushin 22,25,26,28,36,44,70,82,111,115,116,118,119,128,
130,148;
V. Polyakov 4,11,13,16,17,19,23,38;
A. Volkov 8,149;
D. Zamurovic 125-127.

Typeset by Avalon, London
Colour separation by Studio Villa
Printed and bound by Delo – Tiskarna d.d., Ljubljana

RUSSIA
LAND AND PEOPLE

CONTENTS

A Country on Two Continents

The Russian Federation is the largest country in the world, covering 6.5 million square miles or over one ninth of the land surface of the globe. A train journey from its European frontier to its Asiatic seaboard, almost 6,000 miles away, takes a whole week. Even by plane this is a nine- or ten-hour trip, passing through nine time zones. On the long journey from Moscow to Vladivostok on the Trans-Siberian Railway, the traveller will pass through seemingly endless forests, mainly birch and coniferous, known as the taiga, stretching from north European Russia right across Siberia.

Much of European Russia and southern Siberia comprises a vast rolling plain, the steppes, with an average altitude of 650 ft. Russia's greatest river, the Volga, rises north of Moscow and flows south through the steppes for 2,190 miles, entering the Caspian Sea through its huge delta. At Volgograd (formerly Stalingrad) it is joined by another mighty river, the Don. West of the Caspian rise the Caucasus, the highest mountains in the Russian Federation (over 18,000 ft), shared with the Republic of Georgia.

The first real highlands on the west-east trans-Siberian route are the Urals, a legendary source of immense mineral wealth, which mark the boundary between Europe and Asia. Though rising to little more than 6,000 ft, they stretch north-south for some 1,200 miles and for centuries presented a formidable barrier to Russia's eastward expansion. The railway passes through one of the few gaps in the chain and enters the Siberian plain, an infinity of mostly flat marshy land, flooded or frozen bog, depending on the season, where forests give way to stunted trees, bushes and coarse grass, the region known as the tundra.

This is a land of innumerable lakes and great rivers, such as the Ob, Yenisey and Lena, all more than 1,800 miles in length. The Trans-Siberian Railway crosses both the Ob and the Yenisey on its way to Baikal, 400 miles in length, one of the world's biggest and deepest lakes, and also one of the most beautiful, though threatened by industrial pollution. South of the railway rise the Altai Mts, with peaks of over 10,000 ft, which extend into the Republic of Kazakhstan, formerly part of the USSR, and the Republic of Mongolia. Further on the train passes through the valley of the mighty Amur River, which forms the border with China, before reaching its final destination, Vladivostok, on the Sea of Japan.

Beyond the Lena lies the region known as the Far East, with a coastline of 5,600 miles, stretching from the Arctic Circle down to sub-tropical Ussuriland. The huge Kamchatka peninsula is famed for its amazing geysers and towering active volcanoes, the highest of which is Mt Kluchevskaya (15,584 ft).

Those who prefer boats to trains can travel north-south from St Petersburg on the Baltic Sea through Karelia along the rivers, lakes (Ladoga and Onega) and canals that connect it with Moscow, and further south along the Volga to the Caspian.

1. Smolensk: part of the city walls (16th/17th century) which have survived the devastation of many wars (previous pages). First mentioned in 882, Smolensk, on the Dnieper River, is one of the oldest Russian cities. For centuries it passed forward and back between Poland/Lithuania and Russia, which finally captured it in 1654. It was the scene of several major battles during both the Napoleonic invasion and World War II.

2–5. Idyllic scenes from the Russian North, a land of countless lakes and endless forests, most of which has so far managed to escape pollution.

6. No Russian landscape seems complete without a church with an onion dome. Scenes like this (overleaf) have inspired the country's greatest landscape painters such as Isaak Levitan and Alexei Savrasov.

7, 9. Peaks of the Caucasus Mountains, the highest range in the Russian Federation. The border with the Republic of Georgia runs through them, north-south, down to the Caspian Sea. Above: the Caucasus ski resort of Dombay.

8. The conical summit of Mount Vilyui in the southern range of the Kamchatka peninsula, which has 160 volcanoes, over 30 of them very active, and innumerable geysers. Part of the Pacific Rim, Kamchatka suffers frequent earthquakes.

10. Mountain tundra in north-east Siberia during the brief summer thaw (overleaf).

ОСТИНИЦА РОССИ

11. St Basil's Cathedral on Red Square, built by Ivan IV the Terrible to commemorate the conquest of Kazan and its Tatar khanate in 1552. The victory occurred on the feast of the Intercession of the Virgin (Pokrov), to which the church is officially dedicated. St Basil (Vassily) was a revered 'holy fool' who was interred in its walls soon after its construction. The eight cupolas around the central spire, each one different, correspond to eight chapels within, said to represent the eight attempts to capture Kazan.

Moscow and Medieval Russia

In 1156 Prince Yury Dolgoruky ('The Long-armed'), ruler of Vladimir-Suzdal, raised a wooden fortification on the site of the present Kremlin, and is thus considered the founder of Moscow. By that time the first Russian state, Kievan Rus, founded in 880 and ruled for some 200 years by descendants of the Viking prince Rurik, had split into a dozen small realms whose princes were constantly struggling for supremacy. The great cities of those days were Kiev and Novgorod; Moscow was but a minor outpost.

In the early thirteenth century the Mongols swept across Russia, leaving death and devastation in their wake. After the destruction of Kiev by the Mongols under Batu Khan in 1237, all the Russian lands except the rich mercantile Republic of Novgorod in the far north recognised the rule of the 'Golden Horde', the western part of the Mongol Empire, which had its capital at Sarai on the middle Volga. The Mongols, converts to Islam, did not much interfere in the affairs of their Russian subjects, leaving the princes to collect the heavy taxes they imposed.

In the latter half of the thirteenth century, Moscow, favourably located on trade routes, became the centre of an expanding principality. Its rulers proved adept at winning favour with the khans and Prince Ivan I Kalita ('Moneybags', 1325-41) was the first Muscovite ruler be accorded the right to collect taxes from other princes and hold the title of Grand Prince. Moscow's importance was further enhanced by the move to the city from Vladimir of the Metropolitan of All Russia, as the head of the Russian Church was then styled.

The 'Mongol yoke' was finally thrown off in the reign of Ivan III the Great (1462-1505), who greatly expanded the Muscovite realm. After marrying the niece of the last Byzantine emperor, he adopted the imperial double-headed eagle as his emblem and the title of tsar.

By the time Ivan IV was crowned, in 1547, he was quite justified in assuming the title Tsar of All the Russias. Ivan, known as the Terrible, was an unpredictable and cruel autocrat, but he greatly expanded Russian territory to the south and beyond the Urals. In a fit of rage Ivan had struck dead his elder son, so that he was succeeded by his weak-minded second son, Fedor, the last of the ancient Rurikid dynasty. Boris Godunov, Fedor's brother-in-law, was then elected tsar by the boyars (nobility). His reign (1598-1605) was marked by foreign threats and internal rebellions, inaugurating a chaotic period in Russian history known as the Time of Troubles, when Russia was invaded by Poland and Sweden.

The problem of succession was settled in 1613 by the election to the throne of the boyar Michael Romanov, whose descendants ruled Russia until 1917. During the seventeenth century the empire expanded westward, incorporating part of the Ukraine, and across Siberia, with the first settlements being founded on the eastern seaboard in 1649.

12. Moscow's Red Square at night (overleaf) with buildings spanning five centuries. On the right, the red brick walls of the Kremlin, raised by Grand Prince Ivan III the Great when he reconstructed the citadel (1485-95), with the Saviour Gate and tower, its main entrance. Behind, the Great Kremlin Palace, and in front, Lenin's mausoleum. Near St Basil's is the monument to Prince Pozharsky and Kuzma Minin, leaders of the forces that drove the Poles from Moscow in 1612. On the left: the GUM department store and Hotel Rossiya.

РОССИЯ

13. View of the Kremlin from the Moskva River with the Great Kremlin Palace (centre), built in the first half of the 19th century as the Moscow residence of the tsars. On the right, the bell-tower known as Ivan the Great, for centuries Moscow's tallest structure, rises above the Kremlin cathedrals.

14. The Cathedral of the Kazan Virgin on Red Square, originally built in the mid 17th century by Prince Dmitri Pozharsky (see ill. 12) to mark the end of the Time of Troubles. It was demolished in the 1930s and reconstructed in the early 1990s.

15. The lovely 15th-century cathedrals of the Annunciation (centre) and the Assumption (left) on Cathedral Square within the Kremlin, which has two other cathedrals, dedicated to the Archangel Michael and the Twelve Apostles, and other smaller churches.

16. The cupolas of the Terem Palace (overleaf) are all that can be seen from outside of this ancient royal residence, which was incorporated in the Great KremlinPalace built for Nicholas I.

17. Entrance to the Exhibition of Soviet Economic Achievements, now renamed the All-Russia Exhibition Centre, in Moscow. Above the arch: one of the most famous examples of Socialist Realist sculpture, The Worker and the Collective Farmer by Vera Mukhina, commissioned for the Soviet Pavilion at the 1937 World Exposition in Paris.

18. Moscow's Metro, begun in the 1930s and still being extended, is the most efficient form of public transport in the capital, though becoming over-crowded. Its stations, lavishly decorated with marble, mosaics, statuary and chandeliers, were intended as 'people's palaces'.

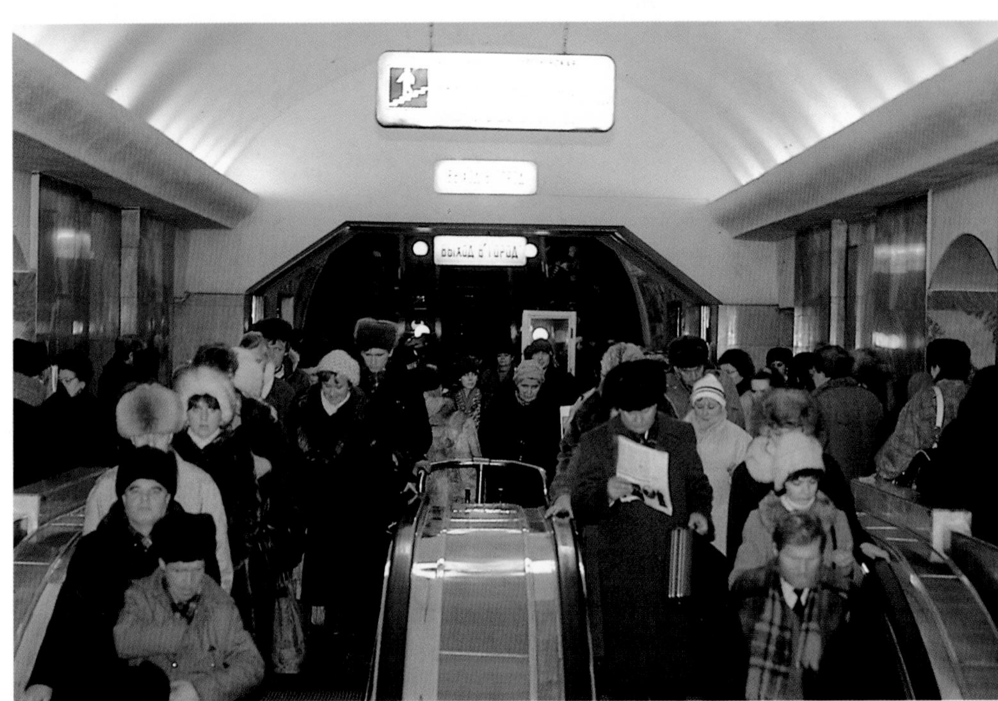

19. The New Arbat Avenue is popularly known in Moscow as the Set of Dentures. To build it, a vast swathe of the old city was demolished. In the distance: one of the wedding-cake skyscrapers in the grandiose style, reminiscent of Gothic cathedrals, favoured by Stalin.

20. Muscovites spend much of their free time, weather permitting, in the city's parks and on the banks of the Moskva. Soldiers and pensioners cannot afford to frequent cafés and restaurants and families like to escape for a while from their cramped flats.

21. The huge Trinity-Sergius (Troitse-Sergiev) Monastery at Sergiev Posad (formerly Zagorsk) has for centuries been a centre of the Russian Orthodox faith. On the right: the monastery's oldest church, Holy Trinity (1422), its interior decorated by one of Russia's greatest ikon and fresco painters, the monk Andrei Rublev.

Churches and Monasteries

When Prince Vladimir of Kiev adopted Christianity for himself and his subjects in 988, Russia took not only the faith but also church architecture from Constantinople. A problem arose, however, when the shallow, saucer-shaped domes suited to the Byzantine climate collapsed under the weight of snow. It was in Novgorod or Pskov that the characteristic Russian onion dome took shape in the twelfth century.

Close contact with Byzantium was severed in the thirteenth century by the Mongol invasion. When Grand Prince Ivan III the Great decided to reconstruct the Moscow Kremlin in the 15th century, he turned to Italian architects, who introduced a Renaissance element that is found in many Russian churches.

The first churches were mostly built of wood on a simple square plan. Later stone churches generally followed the same basic pattern, but were often very elaborate, with as many as twelve brightly coloured domes. For most foreigners, the archetypal Russian church is St Basil's in Moscow, with nine domes, built by Ivan the Terrible to commemorate his victory over the Moslem Tatars at Kazan. (From this time dates the Russian custom of putting a crescent, symbol of Islam, beneath the cross surmounting churches.) St Basil's, however, is a unique hybrid in style, combining the multi-domed church with the tower or tent church.

In the late seventeenth century Moscow adopted and adapted elements of the baroque, creating a colourful, highly decorative style of its own. But it was not until the construction of St Petersburg that some Russian churches began to follow Western architectural forms more closely and spires were introduced. The first of these was raised on the Peter and Paul Cathedral within the St Petersburg fortress. Throughout much of the eighteenth century magnificent baroque and rococo churches and palaces were built in and around the city, many of them by the Italian architect Rastrelli, engaged by the extravagant Empress Elizabeth to beautify the new capital.

Under Catherine the Great, a more sober neo-classical style was adopted, reminiscent of imperial Rome, as befitted a country which had become a great empire. German, French and Italian architects were joined by a growing number of Russians. Though colourful buildings in neo-Gothic and eclectic styles were also raised, from this time on classicism predominated.

From early medieval times the appeal of monastic life was strong in Russia. Thousands of monasteries are scattered across the country, many in remote areas, like the huge Solovetsky Monastery founded in the far north in the fifteenth century. Surrounded by mighty walls and towers, these fulfilled a dual purpose as civilising missions and as fortified outposts of empire, the monks ever ready to take up arms against invaders and marauders. A few of the many monasteries closed after the Revolution have now been reopened.

22. Donskoi Monastery was founded in the 16th century as part of the ring of fortifications around Moscow to defend the city from Tatar attack. Its Old Cathedral, dedicated to the ikon of the Virgin of the Don, has rows of small ornamental gables ('kokoshniki') typical of Moscow churches of this period.

23. Troitse-Sergiev Monastery, 40 miles north-east of Moscow, was founded in the 14th century by Sergei of Radonezh, the 'peasant saint' of Russia, who united the Russian princes against the Tatars at the battle of Kulikovo (1380).

24. Cathedral of St Demetrius (Dimtri) at Vladimir, 12th century, one of the earliest stone churches in Russia. The upper part of its limestone façade is covered with bas-relief carvings of religious, historical and legendary figures.

25. Church of the Prophet Elijah, built in the middle of the 17th century by the merchants of Yaroslavl, an historic town north-east of Moscow, at that time a prosperous centre of commerce on the Volga.

26. Novgorod: the Cathedral of St Sophia, one of the finest examples of early Russian architecture. Built in the mid 11th century and modelled on the church of the same name in Kiev, it stands within the kremlin on the bank of the Volkhov River. The city of Novgorod was one of the greatest trading centres of eastern Europe and ruled an extensive republic until conquered by Muscovy in the 15th century. Its many historic buildings were badly damaged in World War II, but have been restored.

27. The 16th-century Cathedral of the Nativity on Cathedral Hill in Kargopol, a city on the Onega River in the region of Arkangelsk (Archangel).

28. Church of the Ascension in Romanovo-Borisoglebsk, one of the fortified towns that make up the 'Golden Ring' of historic cities in the north-east of what was formerly the principality of Muscovy. The town, named after the first Russian saints, Boris and Gleb, originated as a fortress for defence against the Tatars in the 16th century.

29. Vladimir: the magnificent 12th-century Cathedral of the Assumption, which served as a model for the Assumption Cathedral in the Moscow Kremlin. The city of Vladimir on the Klyazma River was founded in 1108 by Grand Prince Vladimir II Monomakh. In 1157, his grandson, Andrei Bogolyubsky, moved his capital here from Kiev and raised this cathedral, which has frescoes by Andrei Rublev, Russia's most famous ikon-painter.

30. The domical forms of Byzantine architecture were ingeniously copied in wood by Russian carpenters, using a type of aspen shingle ('lemekh') that resembles fish scales.

31. The astonishing wooden Transfiguration Church on Kizhi Island in Lake Onega, Karelia, has 22 domes ascending to a height of 37 metres.

32. Troitse-Sergiev Monastery in the town of Sergiev Posad (Zagorsk). Monasteries, which served as educational and medical centres as well as fortifications in troubled times, were often the nucleus around which settlements grew up.

33. Monasteries were usually built beside a river or lake, which supplied the fish needed for the numerous fast days. This one, founded in 1520 on an island in the Siya River in the Arkhangelsk region, also used water as a means of protection from sudden attack.

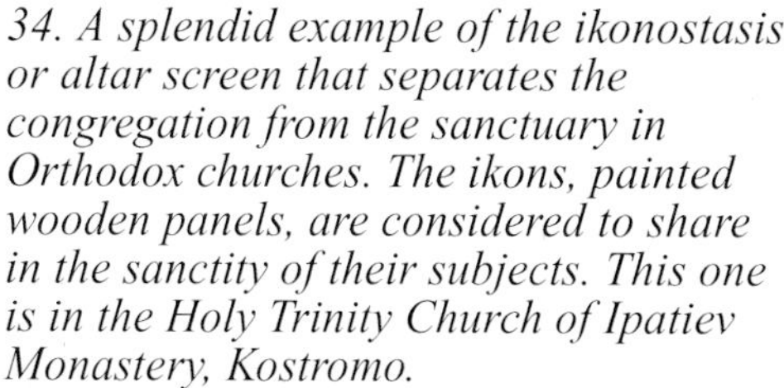

34. A splendid example of the ikonostasis or altar screen that separates the congregation from the sanctuary in Orthodox churches. The ikons, painted wooden panels, are considered to share in the sanctity of their subjects. This one is in the Holy Trinity Church of Ipatiev Monastery, Kostromo.

35. Orthodox churches have no statues ('graven images'), but all the interior surfaces are decorated with fresco paintings. These had an instructional as well as a decorative purpose, representing biblical scenes and saints' lives for the illiterate congregation. Here, the interior of the cathedral dedicated to the Virgin of Smolensk of New Maidens Convent in Moscow.

МОСКВА-183

St Petersburg and the Imperial Age

36. St Isaac's Cathedral, its dome with the lantern rising over 300 feet, dominates central St Petersburg. Everything is on the grand scale: each column of its façade weighs 114 tons. Begun in 1818, it was designed by a Frenchman, Montferrand, and took over 40 years to build. The ornate interior is richly decorated with precious stones, gold, malachite and porphyry.

37. The Catherine Palace at Tsarskoe Selo (Pushkin), just south of St Petersburg, built by the architect Rastrelli as a summer residence for Empress Elizabeth, and named after her mother, Peter the Great's second wife, who reigned briefly as Catherine I. This baroque masterpiece, set in a beautiful park, was intended to rival Versailles.

38. The Winter Palace in St Petersburg (overleaf), one side facing the Neva and the other the majestic Palace Square, is the fourth palace on this site. Another grand project of Elizabeth and Rastrelli, completed in 1762, it was subsequently extended by Catherine the Great, who built the adjoining Hermitage. It is now the Hermitage Museum, housing one of the world's greatest art collections.

Russia's second largest city, St Petersburg was founded in 1703 on the marshy delta of the Neva where it flows into the Baltic Sea. This inauspicious site, recently captured from the Swedes, was chosen by its creator, Peter the Great, to give Russia a 'window on the West'. A giant of a man in every sense, Peter's mission was to drag Russia out of the Middle Ages and make it a great military, naval and economic power. He turned his back on conservative, 'Asiatic' Moscow, drawing on western technical advances and experts to modernise his state.

The building of St Petersburg, personally supervised by the Emperor, was carried out under the most difficult conditions of climate and terrain with forced peasant labour, at enormous cost in materials and human suffering, but within only ten years it was ready to serve as the new capital. The reluctant court and nobility were obliged to move from Moscow and build themselves palaces there, along its innumerable waterways. By the time Peter died, aged only fifty-two, in 1725, St Petersburg was a flourishing city. Under his successors it was embellished with the magnificent squares, palaces, churches and public buildings that make it a unique architectural treasure.

The eighteenth century was the age of colourful empresses and insignificant emperors. Most remarkable was Catherine II the Great (1762-96), a minor German princess who was placed on the throne by a coup that disposed of her unpopular husband, Peter III, a great nephew of Peter the Great. A woman of great intelligence, determination and political acumen, she was wise in her choice of advisors and generals (many of them current or former lovers) and expanded her empire, mostly at the expense of Poland and Turkey.

The reign of Alexander I (1801-1825) saw the rise of Russia's political influence in Europe. After the Napoleonic invasion and Moscow's devastation by fire (1812), so brilliantly described in Tolstoi's novel 'War and Peace', the French Army was decimated during its disastrous winter retreat from Moscow. Following Napoleon's final defeat, Alexander led his troops into Paris in 1814 and played a leading role at the Congress of Vienna.

In the nineteenth century, under the influence of the French Revolution and later of socialist and Marxist ideas, there was growing pressure for reform. Alexander II, 'the Tsar Liberator', abolished serfdom in 1861, but this did not greatly alleviate the poverty of the peasantry, the vast majority of the population.Widespread unrest and Russia's humiliating naval defeat by Japan led to the 1905 Revolution, forcing Nicholas II to approve the election of a *Duma* (National Assembly).

The First World War, in which Russia suffered terrible losses, was the catalyst of the October Revolution of 1917. Nicholas II abdicated and a Bolshevik government, led by Lenin, subsequently gained power. As St Petersburg epitomised imperial Russia, Moscow was chosen as the capital of the new U.S.S.R.

39. The Grand Staircase of the Catherine Palace at Tsarskoe Selo ('Royal Village'). The palace was virtually destroyed in World War II, but painstakingly reconstructed, down to the last detail, after the war.

40. The Jordan Staircase of the Winter Palace is the only part of the original interior by Rastrelli to have survived unaltered.

41. The famous Malachite Room of the Winter Palace, one of the many sumptuously appointed royal chambers open to visitors to the Hermitage Museum, was designed for Alexandra, wife of Nicholas I.

42. The University Embankment on Vasilievsky Island, facing the Admiralty and Winter Palace across the Neva, is lined with notable buildings: the Academy of Sciences, Academy of Arts, Menshikov Palace and Peter the Great's Kunstkamera (Cabinet of Curiosities). At the Strelka point by the bridge, where the Malaya (Small) Neva joins the Neva proper, stand the Exchange and Customs House. Behind rises the spire of the Cathedral of SS Peter and Paul, the first church in St Petersburg.

43. The gigantic statue that symbolises the city's heroic resistance to Hitler's forces in World War II. In the siege of Leningrad, as it was then, which lasted 28 months, a million people died from bombardment or starvation.

44. The Mariinsky (Kirov) Theatre, home of St Petersburg's famed opera and ballet companies, was built in the 1860s by Alfred Cavos, who also designed Moscow's Bolshoi Theatre. Under the French teacher and choreographer Marius Petipa, the Imperial Ballet School in St Petersburg trained some of the world's greatest dancers. When the impressario Diaghilev brought some of them to Western Europe in 1909, his Ballet Russes, starring Anna Pavlova, Nijinsky, Lifar and Massine, among others, caused a sensation. In Soviet times, when the Imperial Ballet and Mariinsky Theatre were renamed Kirov, a number of its stars, seeking greater artistic freedom and rewards, defected to the West, but the company has never been short of new talent.

45. Close-up of the meticulously dovetailed shingle made of aspen wood used for the roofing and cupolas of the Transfiguration Church on Kizhi Island.

46. The area around the Svir River, which connects lakes Onega and Ladoga, has many wooden buildings, mainly churches and chapels, designated as being of historical and architectural interest. The Podporozhie district alone has 64. Being in out-of-the way places, they are less well-known than the Kizhi ensemble.

47. A folk song and dance group in national costume (overleaf) pose gracefully in one of Kizhi's two villages before performing in the summer folk festival held annually on the island.

Wooden Architecture

It is estimated that Russia has more than a quarter of all the forests on our planet. Most of this, an area of about 3 million square miles, is the taiga, predominantly spruce and pine forests amidst lakes and swamps, extending across Siberia south of the Arctic zone.

Because timber was generally more plentiful and easily accessible than stone, and also provided better insulation against the cold, it was traditionally the main building material for dwellings, whether humble cottages or grand mansions, for churches, and even for streets and pavements.

Moscow and other cities were often ravaged by fire because of their many wooden buildings. The great conflagration that broke out after Napoleon entered Moscow in 1812 burnt for six days and destroyed two thirds of the city. When the city was gradually rebuilt, greater use was made of stone and brick, though many of the pastel-coloured stucco buildings from that period that look like stone are in fact timber with daub and wattle beneath the plaster. One such is the magnificent wooden palace of Ostankino, built in 1798 by the immensely wealthy Count Nikolai Sheremetiev as a summer residence on his out-of-town estate, now submerged by the city but well-preserved as a museum.

Few Russian cities now have much wooden architecture of interest. An exception is Tyumen, the first Russian town to be founded in Siberia (in 1586), which has preserved many fine old wooden houses and churches. In the villages, however, timber is still widely used. The type of wooden structure varies with climatic conditions. In the far north and in Siberia, where the temperature falls to 70 degrees C. below zero, houses are constructed with double log walls, with space between them to improve insulation. In regions where the winters are less severe and shorter, greater attention is paid to beautify the houses, which are often of the clapboard type. Door and window frames, shutters, gables, fences and gates may be elaborately carved and painted in bright colours, so that some dwellings are true works of folk art.

All churches seem to have been built of wood until the twelfth century, when the Byzantine manner of building in stone and brick began to gain favour. Even so, wooden churches continued to be raised for centuries, especially in densely-forested Karelia, northwest of St Petersburg. Here, on Kizhi Island in Lake Onega, stands an astonishing masterpiece of the carpenter's and builder's craft: the towering Transfiguration Church with its 22 cupolas, built in 1712 entirely of wood, without the use of a nail, it is claimed. According to legend, when it was finished the master-builder Nestor tossed his axe into the lake, for he would never be able to build another church to equal it. The smaller Intercession Church beside it served as the 'winter church', a cosier place of worship which could be heated. The later wooden bell-tower and surrounding stockade complete this beautiful ensemble, visible for miles.

48. The Sergin House, late 19th century, is a typical Karelian dwelling intended for an extended family. It was moved to Kizhi from the village of Munozero in 1972. Like the houses originally on the island, it was sited on the shore, with the decorated façade facing onto Lake Onega, where it would be noticed by all arriving by boat at the jetty. To create an open-air museum of folk architecture and ethnography, the houses, chapels and windmills of Kizhi were augmented by good examples from the surrounding area.

49. In Karelia and the Russian North, log cabins and dwellings are still being built by traditional methods, fitting together hewn tree trunks without the use of nails.

50. A typical village in Karelia, which has the status of a republic within the Russian Federation. Dotted with 60,000 lakes, the republic extends from Ladoga and Onega to the White Sea and borders on the region of the same name in Finland. Lack of roads make boats the main means of rural transport in summer, to be replaced by sledges when the water freezes.

51. Oshevnev's House on Kizhi. Such farmsteads combined the living quarters and farm buildings under one roof, so that there was little need to go out of doors during the long, bitterly cold winters.

52. The small wooden churches of the north were built for cold, snowy winters, with steep roofs and tiny windows. The example overleaf has a typical belfry with a conical roof set on pillars.

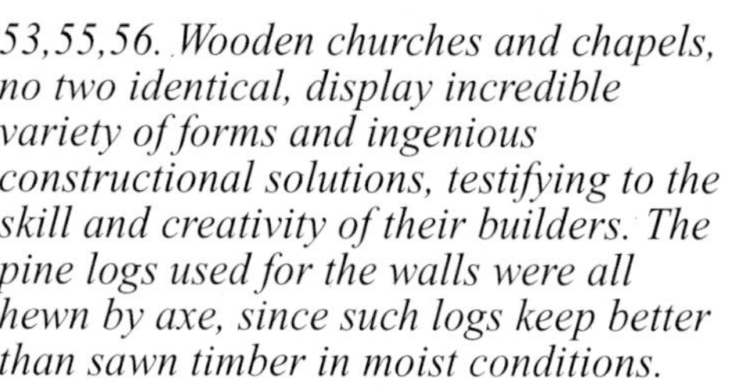

53,55,56. Wooden churches and chapels, no two identical, display incredible variety of forms and ingenious constructional solutions, testifying to the skill and creativity of their builders. The pine logs used for the walls were all hewn by axe, since such logs keep better than sawn timber in moist conditions.

54. The large Transfiguration Church (1714) and smaller Church of the Virgin's Intercession (1764) on Kizhi Island. Behind the top of the bell tower can be seen, seemingly gilded, while the cupolas of the smaller church appear to be covered with silver. This is because the damp-resistant aspen wood used for the roofing takes on a different sheen depending on the light.

57–59. Scenes of the summer festival at Kizhi (overleaf), a gathering of folk singers and dancers from all over Karelia and other parts of Russia held annually since 1978. Local people also put on displays of their traditional crafts particularly woodworking and embroidery, with demonstrations on the spot. The population of the Karelian Republic, though predominantly ethnic Russian, includes some 80,000 Karelians and 10,000 Veps, peoples of Finno-Ugric origin whose languages are akin to Finnish.

60. Villages around Vytegra, as elsewhere in the Russian North, were invariably built beside rivers or lakes. Houses quite often stand in shallow water, being impregnated against damp by a time-tested method. Boat-building is another craft in which the local people are skilled.

61-65. In many parts of Russia, people in villages and on the outskirts of towns beautify their wooden houses with elaborately carved and gaily painted window frames, roofs, doors and gates. Ethnographers detect pagan symbols such as the sun incorporated in the ornamentation. Certainly they reflect a desire for colour to brighten the long, gloomy winters.

1906 ГОДА

66. *Chapel of St Athanasius in the village of Posad, built in the 18th- century and recently restored. This is one of many interesting old wooden buildings in the Podporozhie district round the Svir River. Few of them predate 1700, for three centuries is the maximum duration of wooden structures, however well built, in this damp, cold climate. Dwellings are rarely more than a century old, for families would enlarge and rebuild their homes when the need arose.*

67. Churches and chapels scattered over this area are maintained by monks from nearby monasteries, who carry out necessary repairs and conduct services on their saint's day or other feasts. Monasteries played an important role in the settlement of northern Russia, serving as fortified outposts whose inmates were ever ready to take up arms against invaders or marauders.

68. A wooden church with the type of pyramidal tower that was copied by builders in stone. An example of this is seen in St Basil's in Moscow.

69. Moscow winters are harsh, but dry and invigorating. Children, well-dressed for the cold, are delighted when snow falls and they can sledge, practise ice-hockey and build snowmen in the city squares and parks.

70. This young soldier and his girlfriend may well wonder what the future holds in store. Because of cuts in the armed forces and curtailment of their privileges, a military career, which in Soviet times offered a secure job and social status, is no longer so attractive or even regularly paid.

71. A crowd at a political rally (overleaf). Since the collapse of the monolithic Soviet system, numerous political parties have been formed, some of them rampantly Russian nationalist that incite intolerance towards the many other nationalities that live in the Russian Federation.

City Life

Throughout history, only a tiny proportion of Russians lived in cities. This began to change after 1861 with the emancipation of the serfs, who were then free to move from the land and seek work in towns. Even so, in 1920 the rural population still accounted for 86 per cent. Soviet economic policies, which laid heavy emphasis on industrialisation, led to a huge influx into existing towns and the building of many new ones. According to 1974 data, 67 per cent of the population in the Russian Federation lived in urban areas, and there were seven cities with over a million inhabitants. By far the greatest density of population is found in the metropolitan areas of Moscow (around 8 million) and St Petersburg (5 million).

Most Russian towns are on waterways, the main trade routes of the past. It was along the great Siberian rivers that fur trappers moved and a few settlements grew up from the sixteenth century on. While vast areas of Siberia remain virtually uninhabited, many of its cities, such as Novosibirsk, boomed after the Second World War, when Russians were encouraged to move east to help develop the region's immense natural resources.

The Revolution brought many changes in city life. The large mansions and apartments of the wealthy were parcelled up into many tiny communal flats with shared washing and cooking facilities. Chronic urban housing shortage, aggravated by wartime destruction, was a feature of the Soviet era and is still unsolved, despite the large-scale housing construction programme launched by Khrushchev in the 1950s. This produced a rash of satellite towns and soulless estates of high-rise blocks on the edge of big cities, at the same time creating transport problems for commuters. In the Moscow of the post-communist era, rush-hour crowds can be seen waiting patiently in all weathers for buses that arrive already packed. Only the admirable Metro with its ornate stations still functions efficiently, though it, too, is over-crowded.

In the Soviet Union, shortages of consumer goods and, at times, basic foodstuffs, coupled with inefficient distribution, made queuing a national pastime. Today, the shops are full of imports, both luxury goods and trash, food is in good supply, but many city dwellers find themselves on or below the breadline. Unemployment, virtually unknown in the Soviet era, continues to rise, while inflation has devalued savings, pensions and most salaries. Making money on the side by taxi-ing, street-vending and other means now occupies the time formerly spent waiting in line.

There are, of course, people who have profited, in various ways, by the privatisation of commerce and manufacturing. These New Russians, as they are called, include the conspicuous spenders in designer-label clothes who frequent the smart privately-owned restaurants and night-clubs. The average Russian is more likely to patronise the kiosks that have proliferated in the cities, a more modest expression of the new spirit of private enterprise that has brought so many changes in the past decade.

72, 73. Despite seventy years of Soviet government that propagated communism and atheism, religion and monarchism managed to survive, even among those born long after the Revolution. There are still people who advocate the return of the Romanov dynasty, whose last ruler, Nicholas II, his fate sealed by his stubborn opposition to reform, was murdered together with his family by the Bolsheviks.

74, 75. Among all generations there are many who deplore the New Russia that has brought an immense gap between rich and poor, the reduction or break-down of social services, widespread impoverishment and a huge increase in crime and corruption. In the light of the current difficulties, for such people Lenin, or even Stalin, symbolises social equality and security.

76. For those dedicated to the spiritual life, hope is placed in the Virgin Mary, whom the Orthodox call Mother of God (Bogoroditsa).

И.В. СТАЛИН.

77. War veterans wearing their medals and even uniforms at an anniversary celebration. Though more than half a century has passed since the Second World War, it remains firmly imprinted in the hearts and minds of the Russian people. Of the 55 million people who lost their lives in the war, over 20 millions were citizens of the Soviet Union. The ageing veterans are still accorded full recognition for their military services, though many are unhappy with the changes of the past decade.

78, 79. At the Tomb of the Unknown Soldier in the Alexander Gardens beneath the Kremlin walls, veterans and young people place flowers in memory of the millions of Russians who died in World War II defending Moscow and fighting on battlefields across Europe. Few historians will dispute that the sacrifices and military might of the Soviet Union made the biggest contribution of any nation to the defeat of Nazi Germany and its allies.

80, 81. Russian designers and engineers produce military aircraft, such as the MIG-29, at the forefront of aviation technology. It is questionable how long this will be maintained in view of the economic problems and changed priorities of post-Soviet Russia.

82. The Russian Navy, a powerful presence on the high seas ever since it was created in the 18th century by Peter the Great, is also in a state of crisis. The end of the Cold War and the disintegration of the USSR have made its huge fleet, including nuclear submarines, largely redundant.

83. Once the pride of working collectives and government or party institutions, these banners, specially embroidered for anniversaries or other occasions, are now displayed for sale to foreign tourists at the Ismailovo open-air market in Moscow.

84. As this demonstration (left) indicates, xenophobic Russian nationalism enjoys support in the Church, armed forces, townsfolk and peasantry.

85. A demonstration in Red Square in favour of President Boris Yeltsin at the time when was he was challenged by the Russian Parliament in 1993.

ДЕМОКРА
ИЛИ
ХАЗБУЛАТИ

86. The industrialisation of Russia, which began to accelerate towards the end of the 19th century, was the main goal of Soviet economic policy. Huge industrial complexes were developed in areas rich in coal and minerals. In World War II, many industrial plants were relocated in the Urals and further east, out of reach of Germany's advancing armies.

87. Russian heavy industry, most of it still state-owned, is currently in a state of crisis: workers are not paid their wages for months on end and production is stagnating. The country has huge resources of raw material and manpower, but it is handicapped by inefficiency in both production and distribution.

88. The Russian educational system, inherited from the USSR, places heavy demands on schoolchildren, who are expected to reach a high standard in as many as 14 subjects. By far the most popular foreign language is English.

89–91. Women in Soviet Russia gained equality in the fields of education and employment and made good use of these opportunities, becoming doctors, engineers, university professors, even astronauts. They were, however, noticeably absent in the highest echelons of party and government. Nothing much has changed in the meantime. They continue on the whole to defer to their menfolk while remaining the mainstay of the family.

ФИЛЬМ
ХУМАЮН
ГУДДУ, АМРИШ ПУРИ,
ДЕОЛ и др.

92. The demand for the services of the village blacksmith have declined, but horses are still widely used in the countryside as draft animals and for getting around.

93. To make ends meet, villagers wait at the roadside in the hope of selling home-grown fruit and vegetables to passing city dwellers on their way home from their dachas.

94. A typical village in the surroundings of Moscow. Some are as large as small towns, but lack urban amenities. Rising unemployment in the past decade has induced some Russians to return to their own or their parents' native village, where they can at least grow their own food.

Country Life

Outside the cities, life has always been closely bound up with the seasons and influenced by climate. When an Englishman named George Turberville visited Russia several centuries ago, he described the peasants' simple cottages built of wood and thatched with thick moss to keep out the cold, with piles of logs stacked around the outside. Each had a large stove for cooking and heating and a holy picture in the place of honour. Despite the wars and revolutions, the social and cultural upheavals of the past century, the village home has not essentially changed since his time, though almost every house now has electricity and a television set, and thatched roofs have been replaced by tin. The Russian Federation is one of the most northerly countries of the world: over half its territory lies north of latitude 60 degrees. Country folk have learnt to live with sub-zero temperatures for months on end, stocking up with food supplies, pickles, and, of course, vodka.

Fishing and hunting game are not sports here but valuable ways of supplementing the diet. Hunting, whether by shooting or trapping, is practised in all regions, but in the Urals and Siberia it is a way of life. It supplies not only fresh meat but the pelts needed for the fur coats and hats that every Russian wears from an early age.

After the long winter comes the great thaw, when the countryside turns to mud, rivers overflow and getting about becomes a major problem. Horses, which still play a role in agriculture, are irreplaceable for travelling along muddy roads. In winter the horse-drawn sleigh is often the best means of transport available. Wealthier households may have a *troika*, the traditional dashing three-horse sleigh with its jingling bells. The side horses are trained to keep their heads turned away from the centre horse, the strongest of the three, thereby adding to the elegance of the equipage.

Much of Russia has a short growing season, so spring and summer are periods of intensive work for farmers. Collective farms still operate, but households usually have some land of their own on which to grow fruit and vegetables and keep a few animals or poultry. Family ties are strong and three generations often live together. The grandmother, *babushka*, usually survives her husband and helps bring up the grandchildren, tends the poultry and sells farm produce by the roadside or at local markets.

The harvest, as everywhere, is celebrated with various festivities. It is also a popular time for weddings, in which the whole village will take part. Nowadays, more young people, in both town and country, are getting married in church. It remains to be seen whether this will reduce the high divorce rate, of which alcohol abuse is a major cause. Vodka flows liberally at all such celebrations and is regularly consumed with meals and snacks. Heavy drinking by Russian men (much less by women) of all classes was ascribed in the past to the boredom of country life and the severe climate. In this respect, too, nothing has changed.

95–97. Older women, 'babushkas', continue to play an active role in village households for as long as they remain physically capable. Most outlive their husbands: in the mid 1990s average life expectancy was 73 years for women, 59 for mèn. The average of 65.8 years was the lowest since the 1960s, a consequence of heavy drinking and smoking, poor diet as a result of increased poverty, and the decay of the formerly free health service.

98. Russian shops have little in the way of prepared food so housewives spend a lot of time baking and making hearty soups to keep out the cold. The food tends to be somewhat stodgy and monotonous, high on carbohydrates and low on fresh fruit and vegetables.

99, 100 Winter brings its problems: long waits in the cold for irregular public transport to the nearest town, and shovelling heavy snow to keep one's pathway clear.

101. Beards and the traditional Russian tunic are still widely worn in the countryside, especially in Siberia.

102. A farmer with his horse and cart in the town of Nizhny Sergi in the southern Ural Mountains (overleaf). He wears the usual winter clothing: a fur hat with ear-flaps, padded coat and felt boots. The decorative harness, called a 'duga' (rainbow), brings the touch of bright colour that Russians love.

103. For every village household it is of vital importance as winter approaches to secure enough fuel to keep the stove burning day and night. These birch logs were probably cut in nearby woodland.

104. During every public meeting, festival or sports event there is always a need for someone to organise and keep order. Russans are not the most disciplined of people, but in Soviet times they got used to having things organised for them.

105. Few villagers have money to spare on furnishing the home. The 'babushka' opposite would have woven the rag rugs herself, sewn her curtains and knitted her stockings and jumper.

106. The Turkic and Mongol peoples who live mainly in the Central Asian regions of the Russian Federation have retained their ancestors' love of horses. Here, a father and son on the Siberian steppe near the border with the now independent Republic of Kazakhstan.

107. The number of 'private farmers' as opposed to 'collective farmers' has increased in the post-Soviet period. Those who live close to big towns can make a good living selling their milk, cheese and other produce at the open-air markets.

108. During the brief summer months, herds of reindeer migrate along their traditional routes to graze on the tundra near the Arctic Ocean. Soviet attempts to collectivise the indigenous peoples of the Far North scarcely affected their lives as semi-nomadic reindeer herders.

109 & 112 (overleaf). After many decades when religious manifestations were banned or severely restricted, Russians have enthusiastically revived the tradition of holding religious processions on all major feast days. Besides banners, it is customary also to carry processional ikons, some of which are painted on both sides.

The Russian Orthodox Church

Christianity became the official religion in 988, when Prince Vladimir of Kiev decided that he and his subjects should be baptized into the Christian faith and founded the Russian Orthodox Church, closely linked to the Eastern Orthodox Church of Constantinople until this city fell to the Ottoman Turks in 1453. Thereafter the Muscovite rulers saw themselves as the heirs of Byzantium, and Moscow as the 'Third Rome'. State and Church became closely identified, as they have been ever since, except for the seventy years of Communist rule.

In the thirteenth century, when most of European Russia was conquered by Moslem Mongols, or Tatars as they are often called, and the Russian princes were reduced to vassals of the Tatar Khanate, the Church became the mainstay of the people, helping them to preserve their national spirit and traditions. Thanks to Moslem religious tolerance, it was allowed to hold services and was freed from taxation, so that for the two and a half centuries or so of Moslem rule the Church, paradoxically, greatly increased its wealth and influence. Subsequently, the Patriarch of Moscow, the head of the Russian Church, often played a major, even dominant, role in political affairs until the eighteenth century, when Peter I and then Catherine II curtailed the Church's political and economic power in their efforts to modernize and secularize the country. Hundreds of monasteries were dissolved and their immense estates confiscated. Even so, the clergy continued to exercise a strong influence over the illiterate peasantry.

The schism in the eleventh century that ended the unity of the Christian Church was formally the result of doctrinal disagreements. Today the Orthodox Church is a federation of self-governing national churches which hold services in their own languages.

The Russian Orthodox Church, ever conservative, uses an ancient form of Russian, Church Slavonic, which few people understand. It also keeps to the Julian or Old Style Calendar, so that Christmas, for example, falls on 7 January. The beauty of the Orthodox liturgy is enhanced by the magnificent vestments of the bearded clergy and the spine-tingling choral singing. The flickering candles, the clouds of incense, the glowing colours of ikons and frescoes, all help to create an atmosphere of religious awe and mystery. As services go on for hours and there are no seats, except a few for the infirm, people enter and leave at any time. The most sacred parts of the service are conducted behind the high altar screen or ikonostasis decorated with religious images (ikons). In the past, every Russian Orthodox home had its family ikon, which occupied a place of honour in the best room.

Church-going has greatly increased since the collapse of the communist regime, which severely discouraged religious practices. Many thousands of churches and monasteries were closed; some were turned into museums, others demolished in the course of urban reconstruction.

110. Russian smiths were famous in the Middle Ages for their church bells, which were commissioned by royalty, nobles and wealthy merchants. The echoes of bells can be heard in the work of many of Russia's celebrated 19th-century composers, who also drew on the choral tradition fostered by the Church.

112–114. The Jewish Autonomous Region in Khabarovsk District in the Far East, where these pictures were taken, was designated as a homeland for Soviet Jews in 1934 but attracted few settlers. Its present population of 200,000 is not predominantly Jewish. Its main town, Birobidzhan, is a stop on the Trans-Siberian Railway.

יהוה
הפרכת בבית הכנסת
נדבה האשה וויטי בת
ר שלוס נאטע
פאימאן
תשי״ז
אב

115, 116. Church-going, for so long officially frowned upon if not actively persecuted, has undergone a revival in post-Soviet Russia. The Orthodox Church places much emphasis on ritual and tradition. It was, indeed, a dispute over ritual that split the Church in the 17th century, when Patriarch Nikon decreed, among other things, a change in how one was to cross oneself. This led to the schism ('Raskol') and breakaway of the Old Believers sect, which still exists, though numerically small.

117. Interior of a late 18th-century church much influenced by the Western baroque style. The ikon frames on the elaborate ikonostasis are no longer simple rectangles and the style of painting has moved away from the traditional Byzantine manner.

118. Candles have great symbolic meaning for the Orthodox: one represents the saint in front of whose ikon it burns, three together stand for the Holy Trinity, seven for the gifts of the Holy Spirit. Money from the sale of candles goes towards the upkeep of the church.

119. The Orthodox clergy are divided into 'black' and 'white'. The latter are priests living in the community, who may marry; the former are celibate monks, from whose ranks the higher clergy are chosen.

120. A floral tribute by the faithful below the ikon of the church's patron, which is neatly protected by a wooden 'shelter'. In front of it is a small oil lamp of the kind kept burning in front of the family ikon in homes.

121. Civil marriages are still obligatory, but many young couples now like to tie the knot more firmly by having a religious ceremony as well.

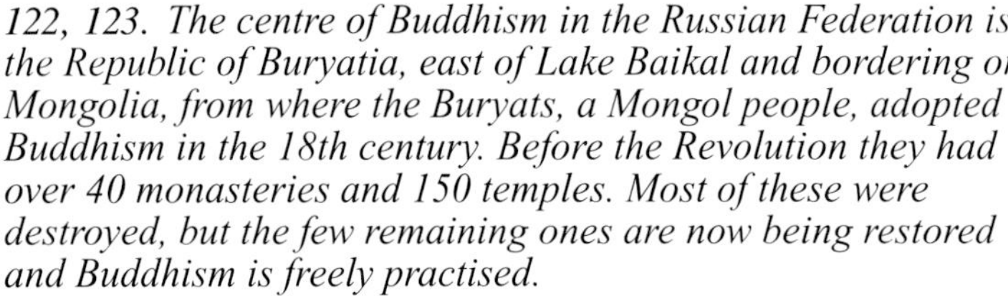

122, 123. The centre of Buddhism in the Russian Federation is the Republic of Buryatia, east of Lake Baikal and bordering on Mongolia, from where the Buryats, a Mongol people, adopted Buddhism in the 18th century. Before the Revolution they had over 40 monasteries and 150 temples. Most of these were destroyed, but the few remaining ones are now being restored and Buddhism is freely practised.

124. The kremlin and majestic 17th-century Trinity Cathedral of Pskov, one of the oldest Russian towns, founded in the 10th century. The citadel's first wooden stockade was replaced by stone walls in the 14th century, when it was an independent republic with an elected prince. Later it came under the republic of nearby Novgorod and in the 16th century was annexed by Muscovy. Pskov's builders were famous and travelled to many other Russian towns to build churches.

125, 126. After Orthodoxy, the faith with the largest number of followers is Islam, which has also gained strength in recent years. Muslim communities are concentrated in Tatarstan, Bashkiria and the North Caucasus, especially Daghestan and Chechnia. The city of Kazan, the capital of the Republic of Tatarstan in the middle Volga region, has a number of notable examples of Islamic architecture, such as the Azimov Mosque from the late 19th century (left), which replaced an earlier wooden mosque, and the Haymarket (Sennaya) Mosque (above).

27. The seven-storey Suyumbika ɔwer (c. 1490), the most istinctive building in Kazan's ·emlin, was once the entrance ·wer to the khan's palace. It is, ·deed, the only Islamic building ı Kazan that survived after the ussian conquest of the khanate in ıe mid-16th century. Its shape is ·peated in the Borovitskaya ɔwer of the Moscow Kremlin, hich also served as the ruler's ıtrance.

128. Patriarch Alexis II, head of the Russian Orthodox Church since 1990. He presides over the Holy Synod, the principal ecclesiastical authority of the Church, composed of members of the higher clergy, which meets every six months to administer church affairs.

129. Baptism by total immersion is practised by some Protestant churches and sects which have a small but growing number of followers in Russia.

130. A procession makes its way to the local Orthodox cemetery for a graveside ceremony marking forty days after death when, it is believed, the fate of the soul is decided.

ГРИГОРИЙ ПИРОГОВ

131. Cruises on Russia's rivers have become popular with foreign tourists, who find this a very pleasant and comfortable way of seeing more of the country than the major cities. The cruise between Moscow and St Petersburg (or the reverse direction) follows the rivers and canals that link the capital with the Baltic and passes through the beautiful lakes of Onega and Ladoga.

Russians at Leisure

Peering out of a window as their plane approaches a city airport, visitors to Russia will notice clumps of small wooden houses dotting the countryside. These, mostly very modest, week-end cottages are known as *dachas*, a name originally applied to the spacious country homes of the nobility, gentry and wealthy townsfolk, where they escaped the heat of the city during the short, but scorching summers. During the Soviet period dachas served the same purpose, except that they were enjoyed by high-ranking party and government officials and other privileged persons. Since the collapse of the Soviet system, more and more ordinary citizens have been able to realise their dream of a 'place in the country', even if little more than a hut. For this purpose, local authorities set aside areas of land near towns which are allocated to various associations or individuals for a symbolic price.

Leisure time is now spent, whenever possible, at the dacha, tilling the garden to supplement expensive market purchases of fresh vegetables, socialising with neighbours and entertaining friends. A foreign visitor will often be invited there instead of to the owner's small and crowded flat in town. For the same reason, it will often be used for big family celebrations.

Another place where Russians combine profit and pleasure in their spare time is down by the local river or lake (very few live by the sea). Fishing is a year round pastime. In winter people, warmly dressed, will stand for hours beside holes cut in the ice, patiently waiting for something to bite – preferably something that can be taken home and cooked. Also with a view to augmenting their somewhat monotonous diet, in summer and autumn villagers and city dwellers alike set off into the fields and forests in search of berries to make jam or mushrooms to pickle for the winter.

Free and compulsory education in Soviet times created millions of avid readers with a wide knowledge of their own and world literature. Recently, though, many seem to have acquired a taste for translated Western 'best-sellers' at the expense of the classics. Russians are also passionately fond of music: classical, folk and pop concerts, opera and ballet all have their devotees.

Sport is another activity much fostered by the Soviet system, its function being to keep the working people healthily occupied and also to create a sporting elite that would win prestige for the Soviet Union. In the post-Soviet era, young people are still willing to put in endless hours of practice in the hope of achieving fame and fortune in their chosen sport: success in international competitions can lead to lucrative contracts abroad.

Travel within the country and abroad, for so long fraught by innumerable obstacles, is now no problem for those who have the money. The jet-setting New Russians are big spenders in all the major cities and glamorous holiday spots of the West. Others look back nostalgically to the time when they had a chance of holidaying on the Black Sea in hostels subsidised by their factory or institution.

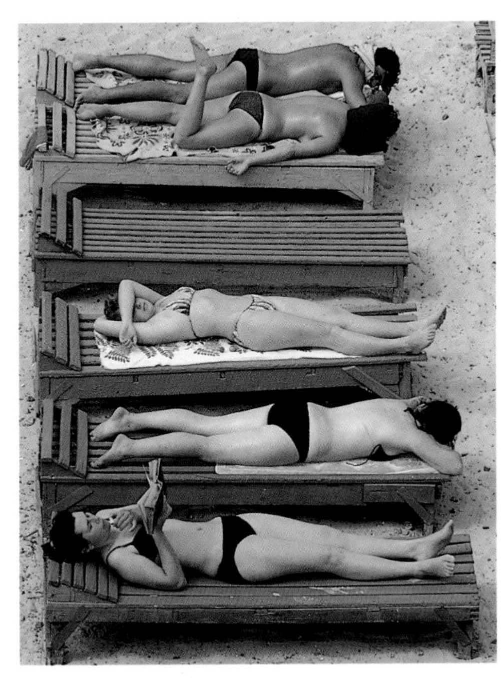

132. Deprived of warm sunshine for much of the year, Russians take every opportunity to swim and sunbathe – at the local swimming pool if there is no river or lake nearby.

133–136. A leisurely holiday on board ship gives ample time for rest, recreation and socialising between excursions on shore to visit nearby places of interest. On the Moscow-St Petersburg trip vessels must pass through a number of huge locks when entering or leaving canals. One of the best times to take this voyage is late June, when the northern regions have their 'white nights' and the sun hardly disappears below the horizon.

137. A passion for fishing can perhaps be taken too far! Factory workers in the Urals (overleaf) spend their free time angling in freezing water.

138–141. Who can doubt that the Russians are a hardy people? Besides the more conventional ski-ing, winter pastimes include soccer in the snow and swimming in sub-zero temperatures. Another favourite is a sauna bath followed by a romp in the snow and a good beating with birch twigs. Traditional Russian bath-houses built of logs are often located beside lakes so that one can leap in to cool off.

142. Bring your own giant drill and bore yourself a hole in the ice (they sell them for this purpose in shops). A box or folding stool is also handy. You can then while away many a freezing hour waiting for a fish to bite.

143, 144. All winter long Russian men flock to frozen waterways in towns and countryside not just for the fun of fishing and the hope of catching fresh fish for Sunday lunch, but to meet up with friends. A bottle of vodka helps to keep out the cold and raise spirits.

145–147. Summer is the time of pageants and folk festivals, which give an opportunity to dress up in traditional costumes. Each region and nationality has its own, but they are rarely worn nowadays except on such festive occasions and for folk song and dance performances.

148. Fish caught in summer is often wind-dried and salted in preparation for winter.

149. A 'troika', the sleigh drawn by three horses so often mentioned in Russian poetry and novels. In the past they were used by the nobility in preference to carriages, which would often overturn on snow-bound roads or get stuck in drifts.

150. Love of fishing develops at an early age. Country lads enjoy far more freedom and often have more spacious homes than town children, but as they grow up many want to move to cities which offer more in the way of entertainment.

151. No wedding or other festivity would be complete without the Russian accordion to accompany singers and provide dance music.

152. *The Russian brown bear, long since adopted as the symbol of the country, is found in many regions, primarily in the taiga zone. Their number is estimated at 80,000, of which some 10,000 are in the Kamchatka peninsula in the Far East.*

153. *A lonely country road in early winter, the time when humans and animals start thinking of hibernating, or at least stocking up with supplies for the months ahead.*

154. *Crossing a frozen river by sledge at sunset (overleaf). A sense of communion with nature is felt by many Russians, the majority of them not far from peasant roots.*

Flora and Fauna

A vast land straddling two continents, the Russian Federation, almost twice the size of the United States or China, inevitably has an infinite variety of vegetation and wild life. It can be roughly divided into six horizontal climatic and vegetation zones, though these merge gradually into one another and there are variations due to altitude and proximity to the sea.

In the north, bordered by the Arctic Ocean, a wide belt of treeless tundra (a Finnish word meaning 'barren mountain') stretches from Scandinavia to the Pacific. Even during summer vegetation is scant – only lichen, moss, a few berries and coarse grasses – for the permafrost is just a few inches below the surface. It is enough, though, to sustain the great herds of reindeer of the Chukchi, Koryaks, and other indigenous peoples of the far north-east. Some reindeer are trained to pull sledges, a task that is also performed by the sturdy Samoyed, the local husky-type dog. The northern coasts, the summer nesting ground of millions of migratory birds, are home to the polar bear, walrus and seal. All these are hunted for their pelts, tusks or meat, but their numbers are such that there is no threat to their survival.

Further south lies the thin forest tundra with extensive peat bogs, which merges into the endless taiga. In these often impenetrable forests, snow-clad in winter, marshy in summer, roams the Russian brown bear – perhaps 80,000 of them – together with elk, lynx and wolverine. For centuries furs were one of Russia's major export items, with sable, silver fox and ermine particularly in demand. Nowadays, hunting, whether with guns, traps or dogs, is forbidden or severely restricted in the protected nature reserves, of which there are over a hundred in the Federation.

The mostly coniferous taiga gives way to mixed forest and wooded steppe with the birch trees so beloved by Russian painters and poets. The true steppe is rolling grassland, much of it now ploughed up and under grain. Skunk, fox and wolf are common here. Eagles and other birds of prey sail overhead, ready to swoop down on hare, jerboa and other small rodents. Predatory carp swim the wide, sluggish rivers of the plains.

Down south towards the Caspian Sea, in the semi-desert and desert zones, extensive irrigation for raising rice and wheat has encroached on the domain of the steppe antelope, wild ass and wild horse. In the Caspian and Black seas and the Volga live the great sturgeon, from which black caviar is obtained. Some species, such as the beluga, weigh as much as 1,300 kilos and are thought to live up to three hundred years. Red caviar comes from the large salmon so plentiful in Siberian rivers and Far Eastern waters.

The Caucasus and mountainous regions all along the southern border have a an abundance of wildlife, ranging from deer, chamois and wild goats to bear and snow leopard. The rare Amur leopard and Siberian tiger have survived in the monsoon forests of sub-tropical Ussuriland in the Far East.

155. Much of southern Siberia is wild mountainous country. Lovely Lake Teletskoe (1,430 ft a.s.l.), lies between the Altai and Sayan ranges.

156. Kamchatka: a wilderness of forests beneath smoking volcanoes.

157. South of Kamchatka extends the chain of Kuril Islands, which belonged to Japan until annexed by the Soviet Union at the end of World War II.

158–161. Winter scenes (overleaf): a snowy landscape in European Russia, a baby seal on an Arctic ice-floe, a towering peak in the Caucasus.

161–163. Hunting seal and walrus is an age-old occupation of the maritime tribes like the Chukchi living in north-eastern Siberia. Traditionally, the eight crew members and the helmsman, known as 'the master', would divide up the meat equally, but the walrus tusks, used for ceremonial rituals, would go to the master. The Chukchi believed in a sea spirit called the Mother of the Walrus who lived at the bottom of the sea.

164. Sunset on the Volga near the city of Kazan (overleaf). Russia's and Europe's longest river, the Volga rises north of Moscow and after flowing for 2,190 miles empties into the Caspian Sea through a huge delta. Were it not for the mighty river, this inland sea would have dried up long ago.